HEAT

Series 3 Number 7

Anna Higgins
O, World! 2022
black and white film printed on
Somerset paper
180 × 130 cm
courtesy of the artist and
ReadingRoom, Naarm/Melbourne

In Edna St Vincent Millay's poem
'God's World' she laments 'O world,
I cannot hold thee close enough!'
and goes on to describe an autumn
landscape with wide grey skies and
rolling and rising mists. *O, World!*
was also made out of the artist's own
form of ecstatic vision, a frenzied
combination of the lines of cloud
contrails, and drawn mark making,
aiming to image the natural world
and atmosphere in a form we cannot
fully grasp.

EDA GUNAYDIN
FUCK UP

Eda Gunaydin is a Turkish-Australian essayist whose writing explores class, race, diaspora and Western Sydney. She has been a finalist for a Queensland Literary Award and the Scribe Nonfiction Prize. Her debut essay collection *Root & Branch* was shortlisted for the 2022 Victorian Premier's Literary Award.

THE IDEA OF A CONFERENCE was a bit of a lark initially. A response to the saturation of kickstarters and gofundmes which, when they saw them shared on Instagram by well-meaning but pretentious mates, and student politicians, Mitch and Robertson dubbed 'dickstarters' and 'gofuckmes' through snorts.

'You'd reckon half of these are fakes,' Robertson muttered. He found it hard to believe that there were so many people with unmet needs in the Greater Sydney area. 'Like is anyone verifying these things?' He had a page titled WHEELS FOR DOBBY open on his laptop and was staring intently at a photograph of a dog with no front legs, who had seemingly raised over two thousand dollars in the past forty-eight hours. 'For half of that amount of money I'd shoot the thing in the head for her.'

Mitch laughed and asked Robertson what he'd buy with his half of the grand they would make if they split the bounty on euthanising the bipedal dog, hypothetically, and Robertson answered that he'd like to buy a legit guitar pick, like a custom wood one, and Mitch thought out loud how nice it would be if he could buy two big tubs of protein powder. Rooting Islamophobia Out Talks (RIOT) was the result of a minimal amount of research, time spent scrolling 4aGoodCause and surveying which plights were enjoying trending status. They'd formulated it hours after the news dropped about South Hurstville, the attempt to light the mosque up with bacon grease.

Mitch had written the copy in the same hypothetical manner in which he had posed the question about the five hundred dollars, able to emulate the affect of the other miserable postings only because he was strung out on dexies, which he used to study but which sometimes left him with excess creative energy and no outlet for it. He spoke to himself as he typed: 'A series of public seminars – no, discussions? No, what about chats? No how about yarns? Or debates? Or dialogues? Or learnings?' He wished he could unclench his jaw.

'Just write talks,' Robertson said. 'You know people donate to this shit but never check to see if you spend the money on what you say you will.'

Then the fundraiser page got three hundred shares, one crucially on Mamamia, another on Pedestrian, sealing their fate. After that people kept asking for updates. Had they secured a venue? Would child care be made available? Tiered ticket prices?

Robertson whined his guts out for days, lamenting having used his real Facebook account. 'I'll never get admitted now,' he muttered again. From his position on the sofa bed, sneaker-clad feet resting on the coffee table, he forced out the opening bars of 'Seven Nation Army', then switched quickly to an Arctic Monkeys riff. This he did every day, making progress on neither song. 'I should have just molested someone.'

Mitch didn't probe the correlation. He had exhausted himself rolling around on the Persian rug that came with the place – their Chippendale terrace was owned by some Bahá'í's, so the living room bookshelf was full up with religious tomes and almost every surface covered in thick rugs. This he had done for a good five, all the while repeating the same question to the black-mould ceiling: 'What does it mean to be unwaged?'

'No, because,' said Robertson. 'Because fraudulent behaviour is frowned upon but – I read that some guy indecently assaulted a woman and he got admitted. Because that's not related to, like, the practice of law.'

'Not committing crime isn't related to the practice of law?'

said Mitch. 'Shit.' Then, 'I'm going to look like the biggest piece of shit to walk this earth. People are already praising me for taking an interest in social justice. Which I don't even get. What's anti-social justice, you know?'

'I guess we're doing this,' said Robertson. He was queen of abrupt decision-making. Once he made up his mind, he forgot there was a way of un-up-making the thing. 'Can food be both halal and vegan?'

'What a question,' said Mitch, affronted. Pausing for a moment, he bounced up to his feet as if mounting a surfboard, then strode into the bathroom, returning with his laptop a beat later. 'I'll Google it.'

A week later, they were sitting next to one another on white plastic chairs whose legs sank slowly into the grass of some Marrickville rental's backyard. The cat that came with the house was sitting on top of the outhouse toilet. Its roof was clear corrugated plastic, showing to any occupants the cat's little paws and tubby torso in silhouette as he shifted around. This made everyone conscious of how long they were spending in there, and so the shits got messy. Robertson, his shoes off and his knees tucked up, kept interlacing his fingers with his toes. Mitch gulped his sour in the hopes Robertson's poor hygiene would stop bothering him if he was munted.

It wasn't his beer, really. He'd asked Robertson if he should take the can from the pile-up in the fridge or not and Robertson had said, 'Yeah, I reckon you should just take it, 'cos that's like the vibe of the house, you know? You deserve to crack open a couple cold ones with the week we've had.'

They had spent the past few days looking up the basics of

Islam on Quora as well as listening to a couple of leftie podcasts – one called Jizz Junction, whose title but not whose content had made them laugh – in order to get a taste for their audience; this, in between studying for their finals for the year.

Mooks emerged from the kitchen with a bucket of hummus and plonked it into the centre of the circle. They called him Mooks but his name was Mukhtar. On Facebook it was only in Arabic these days. It was part of his journey, he said. They hadn't noticed he had embarked upon it at first – in fact they had nearly missed the party, thinking the invitation from لمختار was some guy off Facebook Marketplace who'd sold Robertson a part for his car.

Mooks squatted down at their end of the circle, pulled out a hand-roller and got to work. Mitch had given him shit for the thing for the longest time till he got his vape and had descended rapidly to the bottom of the smoking ladder.

'The Uber Eats is on its way,' said Mooks. 'Till then there's hummus. If you wanna go in for the cost you can chuck some coins into the kitty when you're leaving.'

Robertson eyeballed Mitch as if to say, *see, take a beer, leave a penny*. Mitch vaped on, suckling like an anxious fish in an aquarium.

'Thanks,' said Mitch. He didn't mention that he had already hit his macros today. 'Hey, Robertson. Mooks.'

'Mooks. Mooks! Alright.' Robertson reached out his hand to shake, but Mooks shrugged it off.

'Sorry, mate, I can't put this down or the cat'll eat it.' He gestured at his ziploc of filters, and his other hand which was gripping the hand-roller like an abacus, calculating nothing. 'Thanks for coming, though.'

'Right, well,' said Mitch. 'It's not as big a thing to shake hands in Muslim culture, apparently. Is that true? You put your hand over your heart.'

'Man, I don't know,' said Mooks. 'How's that going, by the way? Have the SJWs descended upon you yet?'

'The whats?' said Robertson.

The cat surged down with no preamble, startling Mooks, whose set-up tumbled to the ground. Robertson leant down and snatched up the thing before it could go for the filters, and Mitch watched as a single ginger cat hair descended with cosmic slowness into the open tub of hummus. Mooks collected up his belongings and surveyed them.

'One sec,' he said. 'I forgot my lighter in the toilet.'

They knew enough about parties and Mooks's often-greenout-afflicted memory to know he would not return.

'You are so cute,' said Robertson, holding the cat up and pressing their noses into each other. He cooed, 'Hello, I love you, won't you tell me your name?'

Mitch had shared enough classes with Zeynep to pause after he'd already swiped right on autopilot, hit with a retrospective glimmer of recognition. He was trying to summon a memory of her tits through her shirt by the time IT'S A MATCH flashed on his screen. He remembered she wore this – this make-up, like she could go off and star in a porno straight after class, that waterproof shit, that made her skin look so smooth and reminded him he hated that men couldn't wear make-up and it wasn't fair because he had acne scars.

'Hey, the pothead from Gastroenterology!' she quickly messaged. She had written him first. 'Me pothead? Lol,' he fired off, then went to fossick through the washing machine. His favourite pair of briefs, bought for him by his mother from the outlet store, were still damp, but he slid into them anyway, confident the warmth emitted from his crotch would dry them out. 'You give head?' he wrote.

'Srsly? Pig 🐷' she had written, by the time he was back on his tummy on the rug.

'JK JK. Want to come over and smoke?' he wrote. Mitch did not keep any pot in the house – the stuff made him hungry, and before he knew it he was capitulating on his meal plan at the Nando's on Parramatta Road. But he was sure Robertson would loan him some of his, the rich cunt. He wondered what made Zeynep think he was a pothead. Did he have a dopy demeanour?

'Yeah orrite,' she wrote. 'Address?' And then, 'Can I bring my sister?'

'Defs,' he wrote, and bellowed down the corridor, 'Rob Rob. Rob Ro-ob.' Rob poked his head out of his bedroom, clutching his Ibanez Roadstar, a prized possession he had bought off Marketplace from an elderly gentleman who used to give lessons in the area before YouTube sunk his business. Robertson had chucked the man an extra fifty.

'For God's sake put that away,' said Mitch. 'Bring me your pot, a semi-hot girl from class and her sister are coming by to smoke.'

Rob's face fell and he darted his eyes between the lounge room and back into his bedroom. 'But if I don't practice every day I can't mark it off on the app.'

'Stop being such an incel,' said Mitch, and the die was cast.

Zeynep's sister looked to be late-twenty-something, but equally smooth and perfectly eyebrowed, and parked her car right up the back of Robertson's in the driveway. Robertson was gracious enough not to complain, only mumble, 'Well, now I can't get us any snacks. Happy?'

'I am,' said Mitch, stepping away from the gap between the blinds so they wouldn't catch him spying. 'Why aren't you?'

He opened the door and, forgetting his training, hugged them hello.

'Hey, gorgeous,' was Zeynep's opening salvo as she stepped in for her hug. While Mitch stared over her shoulder, it dawned that he would not be more confident than her today, especially if he was acting weird and socially anxious and high. He cycled through all the pick-up artist shit he learnt off Reddit, recommended to him by Mooks, planning ways to short-circuit her self-worth before they smoked up.

He couldn't think of anything, so just said, 'How are you?'

'Oh, look, good, good,' said Zeynep, stepped in to let her sister in behind her. 'This is Zara. Should we take off our shoes?'

'No, no need. We have a cleaner in once a month.'

'Oh, nice, very fancy,' said Zara. She walked smoothly into the living room and dropped onto the lounge, slipping her car keys, which hung on a Western Sydney Wanderers keychain, into her handbag, and extracting a phone. Then she commenced typing out some missive, her acrylic nails producing soothing clacks.

'I'm gonna get us all waters,' announced Zeynep, streaming into the kitchen without sitting down. She proceeded to open and shut cupboard doors, emitting slams that made Mitch jump with each one. 'For the cottonmouth. Do you want something else, Zara? Çay?'

'I don't really care, sweetie.'

Zara kept her head down, but did shift left a little to enable

15

Robertson some room to sit. He veered at the last moment and opted for the floor by her feet. She had a tattoo on her ankle which he noticed from this vantage point; an almond-shaped eye.

'We only have water anyway,' said Robertson. Mitch shot him a huge-eyed nostril-flaring ixnay look and Robertson mouthed back, *What? It's true.*

As it turned out, the pot made Mitch loose, especially because Robertson was kind enough to do the rolling for them, which left Mitch with no cause to embarrass himself. Zeynep offered to start them off and Mitch leaned in and made himself the one to light the joint for her after she fumbled the lighter.

'My nails,' explained Zeynep, 'make it hard to flick it. Thanks.'

'No worries,' said Mitch. 'They're nice nails. Fake, right? Your whole look, you know. It's like – very Kardashian.'

He meant it as a neg and, anticipating the concomitant instantaneous drop in her self-esteem, took the opportunity to move closer to Zeynep on the couch. She exhaled a small cloud of smoke into his face.

Zara looked up from her phone at his statement and bared her teeth, and said, 'The Kardashians are Armenian.'

Mitch peeked over at her – maybe social anxiety was kicking in already, he felt uncomfortable showing anyone the entirety of his face, not that it had anywhere to hide, perhaps he would grow his hair out long, like Brad Pitt in *Legends of the Fall* – but could not produce a response. Zara shook her head as if he were stupid. Which he wasn't, because he was in medical school and Zara's dumb sister Zeynep was still stuck in Medical Science, so there. Now who was dopy?

'You know,' she said. 'Kim's always making this big fucking whine on ANZAC day trying to "raise awareness" about the Armenian genocide.'

Mitch nodded, eyes wide.

'Right,' he said. 'Oh, right, right.'

He turned to Zeynep to retrieve the joint she passed him, which he inhaled smoothly, passed on to Robertson. Then he leaned in and, trying not to think about the terrible smell of spit, gave making out with Zeynep a shot. She kissed back after a moment. They were both afflicted with cottonmouth but made do. If only they made mouth lube, he thought, then laughed internally. Duh! That's what spit was. Mouth lube. Ugh, spit. He soldiered on.

Robertson cast about for something to do rather than watch the two of them, so took over the conversation, switching on some of the active listening skills he had cultivated to impress women. Mitch and Robertson were equal and opposite in this regard – they had both studied the best way to manipulate females into sex, but had chosen divergent paths, Mitch a practitioner of old school pick-up artistry, and Robertson having opted for the soft boy, soy boy tack.

In his bedroom, in fact, he kept a faded black satchel he only took with him to his Gender Studies lectures – he audited them occasionally, despite the fact he had already completed his Arts major two years prior, and in American Studies at that – onto which he had pinned several badges that he got for free from the Women's Collective stall at Orientation Week, and which read things like INTERSECTIONAL BITCH; WHO RUN THE WORLD?; A WOMAN'S BODY IS NOT YOUR PROPERTY; and IF YOU WANT DINNER YOU CAN EAT MY PUSSY. Mitch preferred to make chicks feel terrible about themselves, Robertson to modulate his facial expression to show he cared while they spoke. It was a classic, philosophical school-of-thought generational parting-of-ways: Plato vs Aristotle kind of shit.

He counted down from three thrice, hoping that every time he hit zero he'd have the confidence to speak. On the fourth go he finally said to Zara, 'So you're – into politics, huh?'

'I mean, yeah, a bit.'

'Same,' he said. He reached down to play with a tassel on the rug.

She jerked her head down at him. 'Who'd you vote for in the last election then?'

'Uh,' said Robertson. 'Uhhhh.' He laughed. 'Shit, I'm high. I reckon – like, I reckon I donkey voted, I think. Or I copped the fine.'

'Brooo,' she said, stretching out the syllable. 'That's really bad. Did you vote in the same-sex marriage survey at least?'

'Uh, yeah,' he lied. 'That one I did, yeah. Online, right?'

Zara just tsked, stood up from the couch and squatted to ash the joint in the ashtray next to him on the floor, and then took her seat by his side, long legs out in front of her. She leant forward to touch her toes, bouncing into the stretch.

'How can you do law and not know any shit about politics?' she asked her feet. 'That's like – cooked. When my dad was your age he was out protesting on the street and shit. He got put in jail, even. But escaped. Like, *to another country*. And he was only studying teaching.'

Robertson put up his hands as if to say, *Okay okay don't be so aggro*. 'I'm politically activated! I am, yeah. Me and Mitch are convening, like, a conference on Islamophobia in Australia, soon. In two weeks. It's gonna be all about, like, how people are shit to Muslims. That's heaps political.'

She looked at him, raising her eyebrows almost entirely into her hairline. He wondered how they didn't get make-up all in their hair.

'Are you Muslim then?'

'No,' said Robertson. 'I mean, like, no. I'm blond, for God's sake.'

She shrugged. 'I knew a guy named *Byron,* and you'd've assumed he was a huge bogan but his mum was Syrian. It's good not to make assumptions, you know?'

Zeynep pulled back then, with a sort of sucking sound like a bathtub emptying, which Zara and Robertson heard from below, and said to Mitch, 'Could you maybe try just like...a little less?'

It occurred to Mitch and Robertson then that they'd never psychologically terrorise these women more effectively than the other way around.

'Sorry,' said Robertson. 'Yeah, sorry. Sorry. Nah, I'm not. But we're just the invisible hands behind the whole thing, you know? It's gonna be community-led. We're gonna use the Bryan Brown Theatre in Bankstown.'

Robertson spoke the last word as if it were meant to capture levels of unforetold erudition, a tone usually only reserved for when he pronounced the word phở correctly, a skill gleaned from the family trips his father took them on every year before Robertson aged out of the whole endeavour, to Thailand, Vietnam, Indonesia. These days he'd sooner shoot himself than make the trip to Bellevue Hill and spend a single day with Roy, let alone several weeks *Apocalypse Now!*-ing with the man, seeing his nipples, et cetera.

Zara inspected her fingernails. 'I reckon Muslims already know how shit they're treated, though, right?'

'True,' he said slowly. 'But it's more like – a place for people to come together, you know. And learn about the beauty of Muslim culture. Like the headgear stuff. I've always thought that's so great, like, this way of showing you're not just gonna have your ass hanging out all the time. Modest fashions. We're just looking for someone to teach how to do it, all the different styles and shit. Like those videos on YouTube, "I wear a hijab for a day", you know? And then maybe to get a fabric company to sponsor us for it. Like Lincraft or something. My mum shops there. So.'

Zara snorted and commenced tying a knot into the bottom side of her t-shirt with a hair band from her wrist, so that it no longer fell loosely. He could tell she had elevens; the sexy ghost of abs for women, which everyone on the fitness forums Mitch occasionally perused went on about.

'I mean, hijabis get their arses out all the time. It's like a meme,' she said. 'They post online all these women who have these sick made-up faces, perfect nose jobs, fucking hijab, but then they're in like a miniskirt. Do what you want, obviously, like more power to them. But who cares who has their arse out? You're being a dickhead.'

She looked up over her shoulder at Zeynep, checking on her progress, then made the movement into a neck stretch, burying her fingers into her cheek to keep her head turned.

His dad would have called a woman like her a ball-breaker, but Robertson had learned from Gender Studies that this was inappropriate language and was trying to unlearn it. His father may not necessarily qualify as a drunk, but he certainly was drunk, much of the time, only in such a way that no one could call out: chic drunk, like he'd be drinking because he'd been out on a boat all day and you can't drink ocean water or your own piss or Mount Franklin but San Pel goes flat so white wine it was. He called Robertson's mother a fucking bitch every second day, if her distraught emails to Robertson were anything to go off, or the ones where she cc'd Robertson in with the family lawyer, subject line reading ominous things about divorce and trusts. Robertson hadn't studied trust law and it was easier to file the emails into spam.

'Gee, you're hard to please,' he pointed out to Zara. He would have to consult with his dealer on the strain of pot he had bought. He found himself feeling sad, and annoyed about it, that he had wasted an arvo seshing instead of chalking up productivity points or ironing the collars on his shirts.

'Not even, actually,' said Zara. She released her head and brought it round to look at him, shrugging. 'I just don't like slut-shaming.'

She stood, lifted her bag off the couch, tugging to pull the strap lodged under Zeynep's ass out and away, then walked down the hall into his bedroom with it pulled over her shoulder. He followed, if only to make sure she didn't discover his collection of children's books – he had left most of them at his mum and dad's, but couldn't resist bringing all his *Deltora Quest*s and *Selby*s with him. He could just imagine her nosing her way through his shit, but when he walked in she was just on the bed with her legs crossed and she patted her side.

He went over there, half because you don't have to understand anyone to have sex with them, half worried that if pot was going to make him sad from now on then what if sex did too?

'Tell me what your five-year plan is,' she said. He sat down, giving her a professional berth, in respect of the recruitment-managerial style she had adopted.

'Oh,' he said. 'Uh, well. So I work as a clerk – you know what that is, right?'

Zara nodded and made a signal with her hand he took to mean, *Yes, yes, go on*.

'At a top-tier law firm. Like almost one of the big four. And I'm gonna start as a grad there next year. So I'll make like...' He checked to see if he was telling her the right things. She nodded. 'So I'll make like ninety-five grand, starting salary.'

'Cool,' said Zara. 'Okay, well, I have one point two million Instagram followers. This isn't licking my own ass or anything but I get paid ten grand per sponsorship. Like to advertise products like appetite-suppressant lollipops, bikinis your tits pop out of, stuff like that. My goal is to buy a house in the next three years. How do you feel about property?'

'Yeah,' said Robertson. 'Uh, positive? My parents are gonna give me a contribution for a deposit when I'm ready. Also, I play guitar.' This he added to sweeten the pot, heretofore unaware that he was a pot, and that he wasn't yet sweet enough, but he was a quick learner.

'Cool,' she said. She fished out her phone from her bag, opened Instagram, and scrolled him through her profile. She was posed, as promised, with her tits in or out of various bikinis which looked poorly and unethically made, or holding out a revolting laxative concoction, or from beneath a wide-brimmed hat with her head turned away in the sun, or with an arm outstretched pointing at a street market. 'Do you have a problem with this?'

'No,' he said. 'No. Definitely not.'

He wanted dearly to sleep with her, in fact, to suck on her tits or even only to take these king-making photographs for her while she thrashed about on the deck of a boat.

For a joke, he said, 'You've changed my mind. Arses? Out!'

Zara laughed and slapped him lightly on the thigh, but then wound her arm over his shoulders.

'You're funny. My mum will do it, by the way. Your hijab-tying class thing. She gets really bored at home. Sometimes we arrive, me and Zara, and Mum has thrown all the dinner she's made, at the wall, or off the front balcony. It's funny because shit like kuru fasulye – do you know what that is? – it stains like hell. Or pancar. Beetroot. White walls. And she's the one who cleans it up. But like, what I'm saying is she needs to get out of the house.'

The Yilmazes – Yilmaces? – lived right down the end of The Horsley Drive on some kind of farm. They pulled up outside a large shed and Zeynep said, 'Just park in that spot right there,' but it was all dirt.

'No,' said Zeynep. 'No, like, can't you see the bit marked out with two logs? It's to fit a car.' Mitch put his foot on the pedal and drove forward, and then backwards, and then forwards again, pretending to triangulate, in the hope she would give up and let him park however the fuck given there was dirt on all sides.

'Ugh, just get out, maybe,' said Zeynep. He acquiesced, and they switched sides, and she lodged them neatly into the spot. Zara climbed out the back, disappearing into the shed while pulling off her shoes. She reappeared moments later in tattered joggers and then strode away again. There was the sound of an engine and she re-emerged behind the wheel of an ATV.

'The fuck?' said Robertson, expelling a delighted laugh. 'Cool.'

Zara crawled to a stop in front of him, then patted the seat beside her. 'C'mon, dumbass. Why the fuck are you so slow?'

'I dunno,' said Robertson, hiking up his chinos over his thighs and taking a seat. He looked at her, holding a hand up to his forehead to shade himself from the setting sun. 'Brain damage?'

They rode away and Mitch looked at Zeynep in accusation. 'Are Rob and your sister a thing now?'

'Mm,' said Zeynep, pointing at a two-storey house which she started a march towards. 'They just spent the past seven days together, and he's meeting our mum now. Zara even taught him a few phrases to say to her, oh my God it's so cute. Do you live under a rock or what?'

Mitch's prevailing thought was that women always did this, date fucking tall white guys, blond cunts, who they thought were good-looking but they actually just couldn't tell what the guy looked like because their sun-damaged faces were so high up. He was starting to really get what some of the guys on the subreddits were on about, regarding the vanity of females.

'I thought they were just doing prep for this conference. I can't believe he tricked me into being his buffer.' Zeynep only kept walking. After a moment he called, 'His dick's not so big, you know.'

Zeynep looked back at him, her hand prone on the flyscreen door handle.

'Alright, dude. Let's go in the house. Remember to take your shoes off. And no dick chat inside.'

They arrived on the day, after a final week of two a.m. Officeworks runs, an eleventh hour wi-fi outage, and the implosion of their online ticketing system which only Zara could fix through recourse to one of her thirsty Insta followers who had a degree in IT. The car was loaded up with everything they had determined they would need: lanyards, schedules, print-outs on Islamophobia (bystander intervention, Unveiling 10 Myths About Muslims, Best Late-Night Food Joints Run By Muslims – Charcoal Chicken, Kebabs, Falafel and Hummus Restaurants for the Vegans, One Uyghur Restaurant in Chinatown (with a small insert attached outlining China's record on human rights)), Uber Eats coupons, and patterned fabrics suitable to wrap or splay around the head, acquired off of eBay.

They started to walk it all up to the theatre, headed for the green room, clutching the stuff in their arms and climbing up the grand steps that led into the library. Zara was playing entrance music – *Renaissance* blasting at max volume, trying to wake them up, or at least prevent any further talking. Zara and Rob had spent the duration of the drive out to Bankstown settling an argument that erupted when Rob discovered Mooks and her had once dated.

'Oh, sorry, did we have to ask his permission or something? I'm sure he doesn't care,' Zara had laughed, and laughed even more, covering her mouth, after she consulted her phone. 'Oh my God, he unfollowed me on Instagram.'

Rob had felt a sense of foreboding for the remainder of the journey, which he tried to quell by telling himself he just wasn't used to being this far south-west of Strathfield.

'Oh my God, babe,' she had said. 'It's fine! He hates me, not you. What's he gonna do, come to your house?'

Rob had allowed himself to nod and settle, mollified. 'Right, right, that's true. I reckon, yeah, he's not mad. Why would he be mad? You're not property. I think he likes me. I think he's always liked me. He even suggested a name for that last speaker.'

Upon cresting the final flight of stairs they were confronted by two distinct crowds, unanticipated because the conference was not due to start for hours. The two clusters flanked them from the left and the right. Though they appeared to be on the verge of attacking each other, both wore black, and dressed in combinations of cargo or three-quarter pants, boots, and singlets, each sporting hairstyles somewhere between a buzz cut or a sort of funky mullet. They all looked sort of unsmooth, but not old, and Mitch could not tell if they were drug-fucked or hippies or what, but certainly he didn't think either group consisted of their prospective conference participants: they were too angry, and they had made it very clear in their marketing materials that this was to be a conference about love.

They had to take a couple steps back to make out what the largest of the banners read: NO SHARIA LAW.

Mitch had a pamphlet for that guy.

'Racists,' said Mitch, just as Robertson said, 'Fuck, we're cancelled. They're triggered!' He was eyeballing the small-ish rectangle made out of cardboard that read OWN VOICES OWN CHOICES, which the lad holding it flipped just then. The placard's opposing face read, YOU'RE NOT WOKE, BLOKE.

Zara made a beeline for the entrance, passing in between the two groups who were conducting several shouted arguments.

'Fuck you, white bitch.'

Zara dropped the items in her hands immediately then, strode up to the girl, a ginger by the looks of it, with one of those fringes, and she got so close their foreheads nearly touched, so she was pressing her tits into the woman's banner, which read,

LET MUSLIMS SPEAK FOR THEMSELVES, and she yelled, cleanly, 'I will bash you, cunt.'

And then she walked away, casting one furious glance back at Robertson who hurried to follow. Mitch and Zeynep kept their heads down and tried to do the same, but they were separated immediately. Later, Zeynep would appear in *The Guardian*, her photograph on page six, with her face screwed up and eyes red and bawling from pepper spray issued by the local riot squad. The paper's readership would assume the disarray her hijab was in was due to a scuffle, the result of an assault by one of the riot cops or racists, who teamed up in the end, against the smaller crowd, and not the result of hasty pinning into place, using her mother's tips, in an opportunely quiet corner before she joined the protesting crowd.

'A shambles,' she would be quoted as saying. 'I'm ashamed that my own sister was involved in the organising of this joke of a conference. That's why I came here to protest today. She doesn't respect my religion. She worships capitalism.'

Inside, in the small office they had commandeered, in reality the AV space for the main theatre which held only a mixer and an empty can of V, they met in a huddle.

Zara held her phone out and scrolled in bursts – her finger clacked in one contained swoop down the screen, brought its progress to a halt, and her eyes ping-ponged as she speed-read, and then she repeated the process.

'Okay,' she said, finally looking up. 'Okay. Tell me. Mitch. Did you invite a member of Hizb ut-Tahrir to this fucking conference?'

'Well, now I don't want to answer 'cos you're gonna get mad at me.'

If Zara wore a wig it would have flown off she was in such a sudden and pure rage. 'You stupid motherfucker,' she said, before repeating, 'Mitch the bitch, Mitch the bitch.'

Robertson reached out a hand to console but she only took it, faced it palm up and slapped her phone into it. She said, 'Okay, Rob, what I need you to do is draft me some legal shit, about how I didn't know about this, and how when I made that post supporting the conference on Insta, I did it because I lacked – fucking full disclosure or whatever. Like my Hillary Clinton moment. I was standing behind you but I didn't know. Okay? Open the Notes app right the fuck now.'

He only looked down at the phone, stunned for a moment, before he activated and started fumbling the thing around. 'Okay,' he said. 'Okay, got it.'

Mitch looked up at the ceiling.

'What?' he said. He had figured Hizb ut-Tahrir was not unlike evangelism, when Rob had passed on the name – a fringe denomination of an otherwise large and mainstream community. He had grown up in the Hills, attended meetings of the RICE Movement in high school, and gone to Hillsong services each week before he got way into pot. The look on Zara's face was unholy.

'Honestly, this is worse than when I sponsored that book by Jordan Peterson 'cos I had that Audible deal.'

Zara pushed a piece of her hair back behind her ear, rested her head on Robertson's shoulder to supervise his slow progress, silent for a moment before commenting, 'No, no, my password is Robisaknob now.'

Despite the chanting outside, and the sudden sound of whistles which presumably signified the arrival of the cops – God, what if one of Dad's friends rocked up? – Rob found himself leaning back into her embrace from behind.

Mitch watched them purposefully, trying to catch Rob's attention so he would shrink up and let off, abashed like the time Mitch had discovered his kids books. But he didn't, not even when Mitch muttered 'gay ass', just as the chanting turned to shouts and he heard distinctive thwacks like batons hitting bone.

'Why don't you go render some medical aid?' commented Rob mildly, scrunching his brows so he could concentrate on typing while Zara watched, dictating.

GARETH MORGAN
FIVE POEMS

Gareth Morgan is a poet from Melbourne, and the author of *Dear Eileen* and *When a Punk Becomes a Spunk*. He co-directs the reading series Sick Leave.

Riding the Staten Island Ferry

doing the wordle riding
the staten island ferry
the quordle and the octordle
and googling dinner spots
after ditching the reading
at an art gallery where i knew
nobody and couldn't hear them
from out on the pavement
outside, heard boring snippets
like 'kinship' and 'thigh'
and everything is cheaper on the island

on the ferry, the water below
dolphin-glistening like an MFA
i think about my visa options
feel sad and lost
then uplifted by nice emails
good news about my own
poetry, which keeps me alive
especially when i feel bad
like i do now

i'm trying to be more
plain spoken
to figure out what i want
on a ferry looking at Lady Lib
how religious she seems to me
and what sea life passes under me?

the city like a wishlist
we are hanging out at the end
of the world, what
do you do? suffuse
your work with great feeling
like a gull keeping pace with this
orange monstrosity i ride
and no one is solid
no one melts into air

harry calls and i'm walking off
the boat – showing him the island
dan aykroyd and jim belushi
are doing the blues brothers
it feels like a blessing from harry
this is the world speaking his language
plus the call a bonus blessing
we chat about the auction
starting up nextdoor to his place
chainsaws and birdsong

a woman holds Big
and Easy Crosswords
her little red book
on the R train
en route to high dive
to meet belinda, who,
incidentally, i had been thinking of
i'm dressed like a puddle, some
kid poet, so far out of cash

but my talent for boredom
pub's bud lite squared
lift me up like a little novel

a dobby-eyed lady tells me:
watch out, they will come for you
and yeah, they do
and i feel kinda fine

Prospect Park

the banana tastes like petrochemicals
i'm chiquitita in the dog park, pink sea
of humans and dogs

i guess i could have said it seems
like you have a lot of nice friends
rather than explaining my foreignness again

a red bird foraging for my
chemically banana – the light is dusky
but warmed up enough to sit

there are many kinds of sugar on this planet
ludic sock puppet – what sock puppets aren't?
dog people are dull well not all dog people

but this lady who left her treat bag at home
so Bell is feeling deprived – poor Bell...

i part the green sea with my helmet firmly on
and on the hill i climb another hill

Tiepolo in Richmond

i pass thru their tinted shiny gates
like a tired centrefold
to cleopatra's stagnant arms
gone wild and sluggish in reproduction
no struggle in her metronome
yet still it strikes me

gnats under the fluorescents
my face flushes sunburnt

here's my mise en scéne
28 years old, slouching like a teenager
over the wheels of a Zoomo
yelling FUCK YOU to the driver who
called me an idiot
lunch is two dimmies, dry lips kiss and blow
the shining blasé cartography of a suburb i don't love
where work is suddenly Work
but still i'm the voyeur...

o, see you next tuesday!
o, and thank you very much!

Melbourne

i came here because i wanted to think
people come here to think
i love this city, and that love is indescribable
i went up to the top floor, the third storey
of a local market's car park
i got some more perspective, i saw
rooftops, a few of them puffing smoke
and the names of some businesses
i need to think about what happened
i was recently crushed by two long years
and then a bit more
i needed to think
not about the land, that's another story
and it is storied land
but that too is another story
and not what i came here to say
what i came here to say is
naivety has only got me so far
life was like a racecar and now my head
is spinning again up late on the phone
with new york, feeling gutted and blue
and very very far away
on a much bigger and more sophisticated
island. we all make mistakes
history too is full of them
will i grow arrogant soon, with all this
naivety i wear like a vessel made of cardboard?
my indescribable naivety is annoying like that

i started to think not so much in the car park
as the backyard, the backyard i like to think
is a good place for thinking
and i have come so far there
and i have given you so much space
a balcony is a window and it fails me
when i want to think it gives me grapes i don't need
it is hard to say what this is all about
and you are at work which used to be a place
where i would think, and fail to think
when it became more of a performance
so much almost-pointless struggle
which we inevitably fail to prepare for
and do over and over as we wait for the future
i want to give you everything inside of me
it all tastes like poetry

It Might Be Basically What I'm Already Doing

It might be basically what I'm already doing, eating a jackfruit,
overcome by the beauty of another rnb song, another morning
walk. If Rachel Cusk is smug, how can we do better? I'm tryna
find a beautiful sentence before the rain comes...Did you hear
the throat singers on Davies St? Is that one? Wearing a Miller
Chill hat and talking to your mum? 'Ashton Kutcher's got a
brown belt', you said out loud at lunch. I wrote that down.
And then the sea breeze, I mean come on!! The rain might be
holding off

but the Red Bull boys are ready to race –

I met a man who thought he was doing me a favour by saying
g'day and gesturing to another man, saying, 'He must be fresh
off the boat'. It was oddly affectionate, like he'd been there
once himself, though I guessed he hadn't. I took it with a grain
of salt – did you realise we're ruled by abstractions? But let's
not get too psychedelic. A friend from high school's doing the
plumbing on a nice new prison in Lara and a woman is filming
her cavoodle playing with another woman's cavoodle (these
two things are connected; to say otherwise would actually be
psychedelic). And my friend who moved to Philly dresses like
a drag queen now. My email tells me to unwind with a good
game.

Am I when I'm walking up this sentence to my
place on Pilgrim Street?

Am I even a pilgrim or is that too psychedelic too?

ZHU YUE
TWO STORIES

Translated by Jianan Qian and Alyssa Asquith

Zhu Yue was born in Beijing in late 1970s. He has published three story collections: *The Blindfolded Traveller*, *Masters of Sleep* and *Chaos of Fiction*.

Jianan Qian and **Alyssa Asquith** are both graduates of the Iowa Writers' Workshop with MFA degrees in fiction. Qian is a staff writer at *The Millions*, and her work has appeared in the *New York Times*, *Granta*, *Guernica* and *The O. Henry Prize Stories*, among others. Asquith is originally from Massachusetts. Her stories have appeared in *The Adroit Journal*, *X-R-A-Y*, *Hobart*, *Atticus Review* and elsewhere.

The Universal Solvent

On a wonderful night in the summer of 1910, Murdock, who had just celebrated his twenty-fifth birthday, went to visit Thomas Edison's laboratory at West Orange. Murdock's uncle had funded the tests of Edison's railway signal system; in return, Edison had gladly agreed to speak with the young man.

Clutching a wad of manuscripts to his chest, Murdock was led to a small reception room, where Edison waited. The old man looked feisty. Immediately, he stood and shook hands with Murdock. Edison spoke of his research on fluorescein, the ore triturator, the magnetic separation of iron, rechargeable batteries, underwater telescopes, and so on. Murdock listened carefully. When their conversation drew to a close, Edison asked Murdock a question: 'What's your plan for the future, young man?'

Murdock replied very seriously. 'I plan to invent a universal solvent, Sir.' Edison, whose hearing had weakened with age, didn't hear Murdock clearly. Murdock wrote his ambition on a sheet of paper and handed it to Edison. Edison read it aloud: 'I want to invent a universal solvent that can dissolve any material in the world, Sir.' Edison's voice caught the attention of everyone else in the lab. 'So, young man. In what sort of container do you plan to store this universal solvent?' he asked, feigning a tone of surprise. Laughter broke out around them.

Murdock walked home alone. His mind was still full of the sound of laughter. The stars above his head and the road beneath his feet seemed to be twisting and warping. He suddenly realised the tenuous nature of the relationship between himself and the real world. In fact, he had already invented the universal solvent; it was not difficult to solve the problem of the container. As long as he knew how much time it would take for the solvent to dissolve a specific type of matter, he could transfer the remaining solvent to a different container before the current one had dissolved. He had wanted to break the news to Edison, but Edison's misunderstanding had unsettled him. Murdock decided that he would never announce his creation to the public.

Back in his modest lab, Murdock poured a small amount of the universal solvent into a specially made large conical flask and watched it for a while. Then, he took out a gold pocket watch – which had been handed down from his great grandfather – and dropped it into the flask. Three minutes later, the watch had dissolved completely. Soon, he had added a bronze button, a maple tree leaf, a candle, a sheet of paper, an ink bottle, a cotton swab soaked in medicinal powder, a gemstone ring, a magnet, a monocle... He was desperate to dissolve. For a moment, the dissolving objects seemed to show the panorama of a city: the buildings, the streets, the crowd, the square, the clock tower...

The name of this hallucinatory city is LTQO. She has a typical oceanic climate with cool weather all year round, suitable for tourism, sports games and large theatre events. Strangely, ever since the old days, the city has been a harbour for refugees, lepers, decadent artists, fools, criminals, alcoholics, beggars and those who have escaped marriage.

I caught a strange disease during my teenage years. Once I was cured, I seemed to lose my reason. Of course, this caused a stigma to fall upon my family. They had no choice but to send me to LTQO. I remember that day vividly even now: Mr Pyrrho took me to the city in his carriage. It was raining, and the rain pattered on the coachman's green silk cape. Mr Pyrrho babbled on and on about how luxurious and splendid LTQO would be. As soon as I was dropped off, I suffered a nervous breakdown. In the week that followed, I spent my time drinking. But I was a self-disciplined man by nature: I did not let myself sink into depravity. Eventually, I began to explore LTQO, hoping to find my bearings.

I learned gradually that, since the end of the nineteenth century, LTQO had morphed into a commercial metropolis with the help of a strange theory: 'Every philosophical thought corresponds to a specific object.' After generations of study, analysis, and debate, this theory was finally confirmed. Here, in an attempt to illustrate the nature of these complicated and profound interactions, I will list a few of the simplest equations: idealism = projectors; mechanical materialism = engines; Nietzsche = iron hammers; existentialism = machine guns; nominalism = razors; semiology = bank notes; realism = gold; anti-realism = touchstones; pessimism = treadmills; pragmatism = prostitutes; utilitarianism = cooks; phenomenology = maps; relativism = stock shares; postmodernism = fashionable clothes; anarchism = swimming rings; Buddhism = wheels; positivism = currency detectors; neo-positivism = currency counters with fake note detectors; Freudianism = bedding sets; surrealism = wings; dialectics = propellers; naive materialism = bread; Dadaism = champagne; theory of forms = streamlines; transcendentalism = credit cards; redundancy = miniskirts; conformity theory = tights... Based on these equations, we have uncovered the infinite combinations of creation. For example, if you piece together mechanical idealism and Buddhism, you'll get a car; if you put surrealism, mechanical idealism, and dialectics together, you'll get a plane; if you add existentialism to that, it will become a fighter plane; if you take phenomenology along, you can travel the world. Of course, an excess of pragmatism leads to a decline in morality; nominalism, Nietzsche, and existentialism mustn't fall into the hands of fugitives, or else semiology will be in danger; a disproportionate amount of semiology, combined with too little realism, will trigger inflation; a regular dose of pessimism is good for the health…these equations determine the lifestyles and mindsets of the citizens in LTQO. We must acquire semiology in order to acquire naive materialism; in order to acquire semiology, we must work hard. When new thoughts circulate from the rest of the world and arrive at LTQO, they are processed and converted into their corresponding commodities. These commodities are then circulated back around the world.

After years of study, I've chosen to enter the business of Wittgenstein: Wittgenstein = solvent. This solvent can dissolve all kinds of things in LTQO. Because overproduction can lead to economic recession, many manufacturers must dissolve their surplus products and control the scale of production. Therefore, sales of this solvent will always remain high. I have become so focused on studying Wittgenstein that I now consider it my duty to dissolve everything. I want to invent a universal solvent, and I am certain it is possible. But first, I need to solve a logic problem: the universal solvent cannot dissolve itself. There must therefore be two types of universal solvent, and each one must dissolve the other. But such a contradictory process of cross-dissolution would go on endlessly. This question has been haunting me for a long time – I can neither sleep nor eat; I've recently found a way to free myself. Whenever I feel the pain of meditation, I solicit pragmatism in the streets and spend the night in an inn, which provides the comfort of Freudianism.

Every morning, I eat some naive materialism and drink a bit of Dadaism. I keep the windows open while I jog on my pessimism. Then, I ride my mechanical-idealism-plus-Buddhism to the lab and continue my study of Wittgenstein. If I sell Wittgenstein, I will receive semiology in return. In fact, I invest in relativism and reserve realism; I borrow theories of forms and keep existentialism in my private collection. I can see myself becoming the wealthiest person in LTQO...

Murdock stared at the flask. He was saddened to watch the metropolis dissolve completely and disappear altogether. He carefully poured the remaining solvent back into the jar, and – holding it – walked out of the lab. Under the bright starlight, he scurried into a park. Immediately, he was intoxicated by the fragrance of flowers. He uncorked his jar and splashed the solvent into the rose garden. In the blink of an eye, every last rose petal had withered and melted, leaving only a large hole, dark and abysmal.

'Now what will happen?' Murdock looked up into the starry sky. 'It's only a matter of time before it dissolves the whole cosmos.'

Masters of Sleep

Now, if only eyelashes could shield us from time, then life would know of darkness.

This is a concise biographical encyclopedia. The following individuals, with their extraordinary skill and genius, have built a foundation for the field of sleep performance over the course of the last century. In order to better understand the field, I believe it is necessary to provide specific sensory details and anecdotes from the lives of these practitioners. That said, sleep performance is a profound phenomenon, and I will be content if this piece can provide even a general portrait of the practice.

Clive Bell (1981–2064): British national and practised architect. He may have been among the first to practise the art of sleep performance. As the founder and most prominent member of the New Sleeping Beauty Association, Bell established several central principles of the art of sleep. For instance: 'Rely on neither medicine nor hypnotism.' His sleep performances fell into the category of relatively healthy gymnastics. On 12 March 2007, he fell asleep while performing a handstand at Cambridge University. In the eyes of the audience, he stood on his hands for thirteen minutes, then sank into a sound sleep, which lasted for about two hours. Though this performance displayed only a basic proficiency in the art of sleep, the show left a deep impression on the audience and paved the way for the field. As more and more people immersed themselves in the study of sleep performance, Bell's gymnastics gradually fell out of favour. His opponents considered bodily movements to be cheap circus tricks, not real sleep mastery. However, we consider these views to be quite narrow. To sleep while standing on one's hands, or even while balancing on a single foot, requires a significant degree of mastery, and Bell's historical standing is without question. By the 2050s, he had published a number of books and papers on the art of sleep. His 2015 thesis, 'Peace at Once', is considered a canonical work in the field.

Pierre Guber (2015–): A graduate of Sorbonne University in Paris and a former foreign officer in the French government. Along with his broad knowledge and diverse talents, he is an expert in French history. His study of sleep focuses on the control of time. In 2046, he began a seven-year-long sleep performance. In 2053, The French National Television Channel livestreamed the moment of his waking. During this performance-of-an-epoch, Guber was fired from his job and divorced by his wife. Still, a young woman named Jantis, his assistant and follower, took good care of Guber throughout his sleep career. After regaining consciousness, Guber told a friend that he had lived in another place for those seven years. He had married an Indian woman and fathered two children; he had taught French history, and had been preparing for a promotion to school principal when he awoke. Back in the real world, Guber suffered from serious depression. In 2054, he attempted suicide by slitting his wrists; luckily, he was found and saved before it was too late. One year later, he travelled to India alone and became a French language teacher at an obscure university. He married an Indian woman in 2058. One might say that Guber has led an ordinary life since waking, and that he no longer practises the art of sleep performance. However, some people believe that his performance is ongoing: his journey to India was in fact a journey back to his dreams.

Hegel Strom (1988–2039): A mysterious eccentric. He was a mathematician, poet, and criminal. He authored a monumental work, *The World View of Mathematics*; he also served time in jail for child sexual abuse. In 2039, the same year he was released from prison, he conducted the first horror performance in the history of sleep. He placed a king-sized bed in a tiger cage and slept in the company of two hungry female tigers. What followed was the most significant tragedy in the history of sleep performance. Hegel's thunderous snoring frightened the two tigers, and they responded by attacking him viciously. He was mauled to death, his body torn to pieces. He thus became the first – though hardly the last – person to die for the art of sleep. The field of horror performance soon became mainstream, a maelstrom during which many talented sleep masters would lose their lives. In 2041, Ian Stewart laid out a theoretical foundation for the art of horror performance in his book *Feeling and the Future*. In his analysis, Stuart claimed that the real obstacle to sleep was neither environment nor position, but anxiety. A man's anxiety reaches its peak when he is confronted with danger; therefore, if one can sleep in circumstances of great danger, he has attained the highest level of sleep mastery. Many sleep masters agreed with Stuart's theory. Ever since, the title 'master of sleep' has rivaled that of the desperado.

Herbert Smith (2054–): Professional sleep master, is still one of the most active performers today. He replicated Hegel Strom's tiger-cage performance in 2082, which earned him much fame. During this performance, Strom was extremely lucky; for the eight hours he slept in the cage, the two female tigers paced around his bed, but never touched him. After the show, he spoke to a journalist: 'One day, my wife mentioned that I never snored in my sleep. This made me want to try Hegel's show. Of course, I kept my plan from her. Now that I'm alive, I can kiss her again!' The most stunning show that Smith ever performed was in 2085. He fell asleep on a fenceless twin bed that sat atop the New Eiffel Tower, at a height of 902.4 metres. He took a helicopter to the bed and sank into sleep only eleven minutes later. Had he moved even an inch, he would have fallen and perished. But once again, he escaped Death. He woke after two hours of sleep and was carried away by the helicopter. Later, when Smith recalled the performance, he remembered the most dangerous moment as the moment when he awoke; for a split-second, he had felt as if he were in his bedroom at home. He opened his autobiography with the following: 'While I've never suffered from insomnia, I often dream that I can't fall asleep.' Smith is undoubtedly the most talented and fortunate master of sleep. He currently teaches a course on the art of sleep at Harvard University. Many students enjoy napping with him during class.

Baron Pasfield (2026–2097): Though he never performed a truly astonishing sleep act, he was the first to transform the art of sleep into a religion. His basic doctrine was 'to live a double life'. The doctrine is mysterious, but this is the general meaning: in waking life, one's dreams are often remembered only in scattered fragments; after death, however, one's dreams are remembered with great logic and clarity. Conversely, though one's waking experience feels coherent, these memories soon lapse into chaotic vignettes upon death. These two forms of life exhibit a mysterious symmetry. Practising the art of sleep, Pasfield believed, could allow people to harmonise and unify the two worlds before and after death. Baron Pasfield often gathered his disciples to sleep in a park or in the square. At one point, the number of believers reached as many as 20,000. On 3 July 2097, Pasfield was gunned down by a lunatic disciple while fast asleep in the square. His religion enjoys new converts to this day.

Basil Bernstein (2009–2090): An old-school master of sleep. He continued the performance of sleep-gymnastics long after many others had abandoned the practice. On several occasions, he demonstrated an ability to fall asleep with his eyes open, a feat considered extremely difficult. In 2041, he and his two assistants – the Atrice Sisters – gave a controversial performance in the art of sex-sleeping. During this performance, Bernstein was able to fall asleep in the middle of sexual ecstasy. If we suspend our moral judgement, we must concede that the performance was a success. Bernstein believed that sleep was a medium for pleasure, and that men must learn to seek pleasure before, during, and after sleep. He never performed horror-sleeping. He was mostly known for his drug-resistant sleep performance, in which he would fall asleep after taking a large dose of analeptics. Such a performance is not without danger, but Bernstein never had to face Death directly. By overcoming intense nerves and excitement, he demonstrated a mastery of sleep and a lofty mental state. This fresher and safer form of performance soon won popularity among sleep scholars and practitioners. When someone criticised Bernstein for his unwillingness to confront Death, Bernstein responded by falling asleep in the face of the critic.

Tulle Gobies (2014–2067): The most horrific master of sleep, a philosopher, and a lover of noises. In his youth, he watched with his own eyes as tigers devoured Hegel Strom. Shaken, he decided to dedicate himself to the study of sleep. In his first few performances, he demonstrated an ability to fall asleep in the presence of high-decibel noises. Before long, he lost his hearing. Hoping to further hone his skills, Gobies applied twice for admission into the New Sleeping Beauty Association, but was declined on both occasions. In 2059, he fell asleep on a wasp nest. Surrounded by as many as 200,000 wasps, Gobies slept for thirty-six hours. When he awoke, he was nearing his last gasp. At the end of the performance, a witness remarked that Gobies had turned purplish-red and swollen. In 2060, Gobies did a hunger performance in the Balkans. Without anyone to care for him, he slept seven months in the wilderness. One year later, he fell asleep in midair, parachuting from over 3,000 feet. In 2062, he stabbed his wife in a moment of madness. After that, he was sent to a mental hospital. According to the hospital registration and medical records, he shared a cell with a man named Lashley, the most wicked cannibal of the last century. Scholars hold the general view that this experience indirectly led to his tragic death. In 2067, Gobies was discharged. Later that year, on the hottest day in August, he placed a specially made iron tub at the center of his yard. He filled the large tub with water, then lit a fire beneath it. He climbed into the tub and sank into a sound sleep not long afterwards. Later, his suicide note was found: 'It is a blessing to die in your sleep.'

ALEKSANDRA LUN
ANTIMATTER

Translated by Elizabeth Bryer

Aleksandra Lun left Poland at nineteen, financed her studies in languages and literature in Spain by working at a casino, and now lives in Belgium. She translates from English, French, Spanish, Italian, Catalan, and Romanian into Polish. Her first novel, *The Palimpsests*, written in Spanish, garnered critical acclaim in France, and its translation into English by Elizabeth Bryer won a PEN/Heim grant from PEN America. She is currently studying Dutch and working on her second novel.

Elizabeth Bryer is the author of *From Here On, Monsters*, which was joint winner of the 2020 Norma K. Hemming Award. She is also a translator from Spanish, including of novels by María José Ferrada, Aleksandra Lun, José Luis de Juan and Claudia Salazar Jiménez. She lives on unceded sovereign Wurundjeri land.

ONE NIGHT I DREAMED I was in the backseat of a car that was being driven by a stranger. Through the window, streets of a city I didn't know surfaced and sank back into the night; empty avenues lit by green traffic lights stretched out in perfect symmetry. The radio was speaking a foreign language, the rear-view mirror threw an unknown image back at me, lampposts lined the way like sentries, their shadows striping the road.

In *A Short History of the Shadow*, Victor Stoichita recalls that, according to Pliny the Elder, art was born when one of us decided to outline our own shadow. And so, for the first time we saw ourselves: our body and its absence. A presence and a disappearance. The tangible part of us dancing with its likeness, with the part of us that gets away, that flees the magnesium dust of the first photographs but is forever in pursuit, curious to hear the story we want to relate with our lives.

Life is a fiction, wrote Calderón de la Barca, a dream. A novel is a dream too: a writer is a somnambulist trying not to wake. Groping her way in the dark, arms out straight, ready to defend herself, ready to surrender. Without opening her eyes, the somnambulist writer keeps walking, keeps moving forward into the night with just one aim: not to cross the border between sleeping and waking, the only border in writing.

Borders are a game of chance. History sets the roulette ball in motion without looking us in the eye, like a dealer in a casino thick with cheap tobacco smoke. We watch the wheel spin, an apt metaphor for geopolitics: the quietude at the centre contrasts with the vertiginous speed of the periphery. The roulette ball will come to rest in a pocket, a border crossing that comes with a passport. Some will win, others will lose, chance will wager on us. *Rien ne va plus*. No more bets.

The roulette pocket on which our ball has fallen is our Plato's cave. Seated on the ground, we watch the shadows cast onto the wall by an invisible fire. The Others parade before our eyes, figures clad in strange garments who shout out in terror in languages we don't understand. Devoured by time and history, the Others, like us, pick their way through the gloom. Stoichita connects the Pliny the Elder story with Plato's: to see beyond the shadow is the work of art and knowledge both.

With each novel we see beyond a different shadow, with each novel we dream a different dream. The somnambulist writer gropes her way in the dark, arms out straight, ready to defend herself, ready to surrender. Writing wants to teach us to surrender. To surrender unconditionally, to raise our arms before a squadron of shadows, their military boots an inch off the ground, their footsteps echoing in the silence of the cave. On the walls, the shadows of Plato dancing with the buffalos of Altamira, with the horses of Lascaux, with the hands that adorn the Patagonian caves, with the human footprint on the moon. The somnambulist writer takes up the ochre; not opening her eyes, she draws us on the wall: all that we were, all that we did not know how to be.

Rien ne va plus. The roulette of history assigns us a language too. We learned it inadvertently, we learned it without effort, its words seem to have been waiting for us since the dawn of time. Our mother tongue accompanies us in the same way that our shadow does. Foreign languages observe us from afar. Some reject us, bark at us like dogs guarding their territory. Others ignore us with the apathy of beauties courted by many. Some fall in love with us. They surrender unconditionally, they murmur sweet words of love that we note down in our novice handwriting.

We still haven't realised that a language is a harbinger of change.

A new language is Einstein's cataclysmic event: it creates waves in the spacetime of our lives. It displaces our centre of gravity, modifies our trajectory forever. Our mother tongue is the fuel that propels us to space; the foreign language, the gravitational force of an unknown planet that pulls us into its orbit.

This contact with another planet transforms us. The foreign language becomes our alter ego, the twin sibling who will accompany us for the rest of our lives. We split, disappear, and reappear elsewhere. We win and lose universes; words are born and die in us like distant galaxies. In each language we travel to a different galaxy: in each language we are a different person.

Rien ne va plus. With our passport and our mother tongue, the roulette of history assigns us the most superficial layer of our identity: a fragile 'I' wrapped in a flag. The flag administers its sleep elixir, turns us into citizens of a nightmare. It lulls us into a coma with its tale of victories and defeats, of one-dimensional heroes always standing tall, always on the right side of history. It hypnotises us with all that it declares and all that it conceals, it shows us the Other: a monster lurking beyond borders put there to protect us from incursions by barbaric doubt. The flag shouts, twists, flutters in the emptiness. The surface of the moon accepts it silently. The somnambulist writer navigates the moon craters, still not rousing, still not crossing the border between sleeping and waking, the only border in writing.

One small step for a woman, one giant leap for literature. All literature is a tale about the Other, said Ryszard Kapuściński; every encounter with the Other is a mystery, an illusion of space. At daybreak we toss and turn in bed, the pillow presses down on us like an astronaut's helmet. We open the window, from our crow's nest we observe the night, we scrutinise the horizon in search of sails or spacecraft, in search of someone who might glimpse us. From the distance of the Fata Morgana, the Other signals to us with a mirror. The Other throws us back our reflection, throws us back the fiction of our reflection.

Our reflection is a fiction, our biography is a fiction. The shadows of the past dance across the white screen of an empty cinema. The film ended some time ago. We remain in our seats; we scrutinise the credits in search of an explanation. The somnambulist writer walks along the corridors of the repository, kilometres of film reel wave in greeting as she passes by. The flags harass her, they assail her on a corner. They pin her to the ground, they gag her, the silence engulfs her the way the sound of a piano engulfs a silent film. Music is more than the sum of its notes. Identity is more than the sum of its flags. Life is more than the sum of its fictions.

Our passport is a fiction. It is the answer to a question that needs no reply, a riddle that has no solution. Like a coach obsessed with his team's past victories, our passport teaches us to ask each other where we have come from rather than where we are going. To ask after our origin, not our destination. To ask after our past, not our present. Not our future.

Rien ne va plus. The roulette wheel keeps spinning, the quietude at the centre keeps contrasting with the vertiginous speed of the periphery, centrifugal force parts literature in two. The centre resides in a luminous mansion. Through the windows, laughter and applause can be heard. A passport monitors the door, dominant languages patrol the grounds like bodyguards. The periphery writhes in the shadow, bellows its prayers in incomprehensible languages. Let us in, it whispers through the gaps in the gate, let us tell you a story. The Acheron's unstoppable current sweeps it up in its path. Translation, the Charon of universal literature, looks the other way. The periphery, child of a language too poor to pay the obolus for passage to posterity, awaits the boat in vain. In the sleeping quarters of the mansion, the light is extinguished: nobody notes the periphery's absence.

Literature begins with the absence of writing. Oral storytelling keeps us company in the caves; for millennia, stories fly above our heads, intersecting on their flight paths like migratory birds. Every form of life begins with a cell. Every letter of the alphabet begins with an image. Almost all modern alphabets derive from hieroglyphs: we are still making marks on the walls of the pyramids. We all write with the same alphabet, we all write in the same language, we all write the same story. The somnambulist writer keeps going, still not rousing, still not crossing the border between sleeping and waking, the only border in writing.

An alphabet is a novel, the hidden plot of our lives. Letters surround us like subatomic particles, the makings of the universe. They welcome us on birth certificates, smile at us from the pages of children's books, greet us on café menus. They take our hand in airports, guide us along highways, pinpoint our whereabouts on maps. They accompany us down the corridors of the hospital, their familiar faces explain the diagnosis. The send us off with epitaphs, disintegrate along with our bodies in the rain. Always present, always seated in the first row at our circus performance, letters are our most loyal public, the invisible ink with which we describe the enigma of our lives.

Inside the circus tent, the spotlights search the sand; along a tightrope, the somnambulist writer gropes her way in the dark, arms stretched out before her, ready to defend herself, ready to surrender. We defend ourselves against falls, defend ourselves against voids; there is nothing against which to defend ourselves, there is nowhere to plummet. Our atoms are empty, the void is our home. United by gravity, we plurilingual tightrope walkers advance across the earthly orbit. The alphabet speaks all languages. The alphabet writes all books.

Rien ne va plus. Chance draws the borders, chance intermingles the genes, the somnambulist writer is born in a country. Footballers tear across the television screen, the flag cheers them on from the couch. One of the teams wins the World Cup, the players embrace the cup, the national anthem floods the stadium. The somnambulist writer is all alone, running towards the goal. The passport shouts from the dugout, the somnambulist writer loses the ball, keeps running forward, the Altamira buffalos trot alongside, the Lascaux horses gallop over the freshly cut grass. The public falls quiet, the commentator is struck dumb. Literature is not the World Cup final. A writer is not a footballer. A novel is not a goal for the national team.

A novel is a stateless oracle, a true orphan of language. Centuries erase the hieroglyphs adorning the pyramids, destroy the Latin letters trapped in rolls of papyrus, rust the moveable type of Gutenberg's workshop. The truth disintegrates before our eyes, fiction disintegrates before our eyes. A novel asks that we look at the blank page hidden behind the letters. It asks us to read the tale that precedes any language: the story our atoms are writing in the language of the big bang.

According to the big bang theory, in the early universe matter and antimatter existed in equal quantities. Matter is composed of particles; antimatter, of antiparticles; the two annihilate each other. In the big bang, particles and antiparticles were born and died together, appeared and disappeared in the heat of the explosions. Matter survived; it saved our lives. Antimatter dissipated. Until in 1995 we created the first antiatom, annihilated the instant it encountered matter. We had only forty nanoseconds to try to outline our own shadow.

Life is a shadow, wrote Calderón de la Barca, a dream. We are the first dream of the mother tongue. We are the last dream of the foreign language, of antilanguage: a love come late that tries to make up for lost time. Give me forty more nanoseconds, antilanguage whispers to us from each mirror, give me one more second. Give me one more minute, one more day, one more year, give me one more life. Don't move, don't go, don't wake. Together we will escape time, together we will explore the antiworlds. In the geometry of space, I will look into your eyes, dictionaries will burn in the night and we will not be alone.

And we are not alone. Seated in the backseat of a car that is being driven by a stranger, through the window we watch as the streets of a city we don't know surface and sink back into the night; empty avenues lit by green traffic lights stretch out in perfect symmetry. The radio is speaking a foreign language, the rear-view mirror throws an image of the Other back at us, lampposts line the way like sentries, their shadows striping the road. The driver stops the car, we get out, we stretch out our arms, we start to walk. We keep going without rousing, we keep walking. We keep on, not crossing the border between sleeping and waking, the only border in literature.

This text was commissioned by Passa Porta: International House of Literature in Brussels for the Passa Porta Festival 2021.

π.O.
FOUR POEMS

π.O. is a legendary figure in the Australian poetry scene, the chronicler of Melbourne and its culture and migrations, and a highly disciplined anarchist. He is the publisher of *Unusual Work* by Collective Effort Press, a long-time magazine editor, a pioneer of performance poetry in Australia, and the author of many collections, including *Heide*, which was shortlisted for the Prime Minister's Literary Award for Poetry and received the Judith Wright Calanthe Award. His next book, *The Dirty T-Shirt Tour*, will be published in 2023.

I Come On

      I come on: No guitar.
No drum-kit. No make-Up. No p.a. (What's
missing?) I come on: Read a poem. Read a Noun.
Make a connection (Make a *small* correction).
(Break / a whole line). I come on: Uncertain about
the poem. Uncertain about the crowd. Uncertain
about the poems. It's amazing how a poem
can go missing in front of a whole crowd.
I come on... Read a poem. Everyone at
the venue's *listening.* I come on: read a poem.
And another. (Something's missing). I come on:
read a poem. And another. (And another).
(Wish i hadden!). I come on. – *C'mon Read The
fucken* Poem*!* – Get a HUGE reaction. Feel *like*
i've been caught *kissing!* I come on: read a poem.
And another. Get to the Airport. – The plane's gone!
Get to the station; ditto. The platforms are empty.
I come on. Read a poem. And another. Wondering
what in *Life* i'm suppose to have been missing out on.
I come on. Read a poem. Get drunk, and
see the night out, ////// walking thru the back
streets of Collingwood & Fitzroy (at night), high
on the sound of that lone '♪' [whistle] that
came thru (for me) (from the public bar).
I come on: On a Friday night. In the middle of
a party. After work. No guitar. No drum-kit.
No make-Up. No p.a. No one gives
a fuck. Guess what's missing?
      no Comeback.

Aging Stars

       This bottle of bourbon, is
playing to the crowd. This could be
a once in a lifetime song; telling tales of
lost love, playing havoc with the public bar...
You do some shows, and you get nothing
for it. You want more of a little, and
a lot more, of it. What's in the skies tonight? / Stars.
$40 gets you up, on Stage (just to
jam) with a few guitars – zero *context* –
They used to say 'Hey, you guys could go on *Forever*'.
We could walk thru glass, but we couldn't
pull our *hearts* out every Sunday at the pub
to the same crowd. Life throws a whole
bunch of things at you. Everything changes.
There are a lot of guys, that play like '*us*' now.
I could stand here & sing & scream, but
age is inevitable. ♫ *Legless days and legless
nights* ♫ There's plenty of *Other* things
that go into it, like a Good mix; nothing *too
much* the same. Kick the kerb. The results are
a blast – or should'a been – It's crazy.
We've been together now for over 20 years.
Funny how it *wrangles* in the brain. The future of
the band hangs in the balance; a (breathing) (mask) (for
the aging Elvis). *She Gave Me Hell* was just
the start. The night, was a knockout. The crowd
towards the front))))) *throbbed*. I played 'my
best solo' that night. I think it's about time

we stopped blaming the *Past* – falling backwards – face-up!
Darkness was the outstanding number (that
night); driving blind (together) to get *there* on time.
You can't really *trust* the Rappers... (There are
all kinds of Hustlers!!) Mr Sunshine, Monica, and
the Mind Readers, Wanita and the Lucky
Bastards, all ahead of the Game – *a 50-year career!* –
Take care of your *insides!* A surgical procedure
can land you on your arse; singing 1/2 songs, and tempting
the young ones to come backstage. Took us from
Heavy Metal to Grunge, and back to guns (n' Roses). (Same
wave, different class). A lightbulb moment 'sex
appeal is just a game you go thru on your way
back to the truck'. Then the lead said, he was going to
go back to playing Frank [Sinatra] and people
went crazy. Beer of the month $6.50. Rye is Gospel;
schooners all day (every day) (all events) – Free Entry.
Big bangs. Babel Fish, and a lot of Doggerel.
We were a volley of bad fucks, people calling out for
bullets to come flying past. – I just realised our
1/2 way mark; was beer with Angus [Young] vomiting on
the Stage, or down a back lane. I'd invite you
to come back to my place... – No thanks –
Generational anarchy, is the lifeblood of the young.
Don't know what actually happened, i just froze
up there up on stage, in a lot of trivia & sparks.
I'm sick of all those clowns & punks hanging around
outside in front of the dumpster, shooting up. – Don't St:
Don't know. Don't care. Don't Give A Fuck!
together we played our hearts out; *Yours & Ours*

69

and *some*. Passion is the survival mechanism of the Poor
until the core runs out, and collapses under its
own weight, like our own *sun* does (each
night) to make way for the young,
      at 'Art.

Strike-Day

We're angry
We're Union
We're Angry and we're proud.
We're angry
Come out
We need you in the crowd.

I went to bed early (listening
to the radio); the walls were still HOT after 4 days
of north-winds; the radio predicted a 'cool' change, but
i fell asleep before it came.
      I woke up twice: 2-30, 3-45.
It was raining *teradactals,* but i fell asleep cos it was warm.
      In the morning: The rain
was still falling; the gutters were plugged-up
with old newspapers, and bottles (floating over
the drains). I started to walk to work.
      I stopped to have breakfast
: bacon'n'eggs. Rebecca was glad to see me.
She said, she told the Boss she was resigning.
It was just her, and the cook this morning.
She said, she'll miss the place. She felt like crying.
      I told her i had to go to work...
The rain was stopping...
      I said, i'd see her later the Trams were out.
I gave her $10, and she
                gave me my change.

Boarding House

Bugs, mosquitoes, fleas,
and flies…Down the stairs, anybody's…
everyone's / Anyone's / Nobody's.
It's not in the Landlord's wine, to make
a boarding house Welcoming.
The arsehole who said that the soup
could have tasted better if *all the dishes* had been
washed in it first, didn't get that soup
in a boarding house. You have to remember
always, to look behind the wardrobe to see where
all the cockroaches live. It's the lack of
contact with people that makes people feel lonely.
I remember walking up a lane 2 in the morning,
an' this bloke offering to let me sleep at
his place. – Lots of horrible shit! –
Isolation, is a room, you can't get out of.
Tried suicide, 5 times. (You have to deal with
all sorts of shit). People look at a picture of you, and
think you're okay. The people across
the street told the Landlord everything in
the background; was stolen. All my family call me 'Idiot'.
You feed off that. And your own negativity.
Nobody understands how anybody
can't eat; living in accommodation and
only $2 left for a pie. When i couldn't relate (like
taking a sleeping tablet) i drank. Who i am is *How* i am.
Hand in hand with tears, and sadnesses.
You're holding on, and (not just family) they're

telling you, the most important thing to do
is to just let go. Lots of people are dead inside.
I walked away with a TV once. (Don't know *what*
triggered that). (I owed money i guess). (All
over Melbourne). (Rent up the shit). (Months of
it). An alcoholic has to be carried //// up
the stairs, to get them to sleep. (They can't
find their feet). A performer is supposed to make
an audience laugh *technically* every 7 secs; sitting with
anxiety, and effecting a broken voice; 'I Don't
Live Here Anymore'. You just have to get on with it.
If they call in a Control freak, you're dead meat.
'Get a proper job!' (playing at a shitty little
warehouse gig). (Stealing music to liven up the gig).
(Being pushed to breaking point). 'Everyone's'
not a good word. Then a full drum kit kick, and
a calculated stumble, ends it all. Repeat.
And the session ends to disinterested
      / //   /   applause.

NOÉMI LEFEBVRE
LES NON-DUPES ERRENT
AND OTHER GHOSTS

Translated by Sophie Lewis

Noémi Lefebvre was born in 1964 in Caen and lives in Lyon. She is the author of four novels, including *Blue Self-Portrait* and *Poetics of Work*, both translated from the French by Sophie Lewis. She is a regular contributor to *Mediapart* and the bilingual French-German review *La Mer Gelée*. Her latest book, *Speak / Stop*, will be published in English in 2024.

Sophie Lewis is a British-Australian literary editor and translator from French and Portuguese into English. She has translated Stendhal, Verne, Marcel Aymé, Violette Leduc, Emmanuelle Pagano, Colette Fellous, Leïla Slimani, Sheyla Smanioto and João Gilberto Noll, among others. In 2018 her translation of Noémi Lefebvre's *Blue Self-Portrait* was shortlisted for the Scott Moncrieff and Republic of Consciousness prizes. In 2022 she was joint winner of the French-American Foundation prize for non-fiction translation, for her work on anthropologist Nastassja Martin's book *In the Eye of the Wild*.

NO, I'M FINE. I'M WORKING ON MY TRAGEDY. I'm not making much progress. In the mornings I think about hope and then I naturally think about the state of the world and one thing leads to another and then I'm thinking about my own situation, i.e. about my tragedy. I think that I'm thinking about it at the same time as thinking about it while thinking that I'm thinking, I wonder if this does me any good, I try to think of what does me good, a coffee for example, so I make myself a coffee and toast with strawberry jam while the French Air and Space Force troops are fully engaged in reinforcing the Atlantic Alliance's strategic solidarity, this brave new day is gloomy, I look out the window, I can see the sky to the west, rain over the city and the tree turning green but can it be serious, all this poetry these days when to speak of trees is almost a crime? I start to write on the wings of birds with the idea of continuing on all the pages read, on all the blank pages, then I lose heart, I'd like to be committed without having to want to be like those heroes who purely and simply act but I haven't the strength. Yesterday I read something about the gods, it seems that in the tragic writers, human action is not, of itself, strong enough to do without the power of the gods; I was mid-thinking about the gods and remembering the use of technology in war as an alternative way to rule the heavens when, above the rooftops, I suddenly saw a fly-past of Rafale jets shooting over from Mont-de-Marsan, our nation's contribution to the reinforcement of NATO's dissuasive and defensive posture on Europe's eastern flank. What could I do? Tweet, perhaps? I don't know, I don't know any more. I eat my toast, the coffee is good, it's from Costa Rica, which is well known for its coffee, cultivated in the shade, product of coffee shrubs planted at an altitude of 1,700 metres, it is hand-harvested on the high plateaux of Tarrazú, Tarrazú being very green and little visited, which perhaps follows, the product is strictly monitored, fair trade, respect for the land and its cultivators, harvest by hand, aroma, exotic dream, all this loveliness kills me. I know a global justice activist who swapped his morning coffee for a rosemary infusion because rosemary is good for the climate and good for the health and it grows in your garden, which is well and good, really very good, only I don't have a garden and I do like coffee – without sugar. I like sugarless coffee. When I think how some writers devote pages and pages to describing their pleasure in drinking coffee with sugar. How sad. Even if the sugar is literary. Around the end of last autumn, while I was out looking for diesel in the Haute-Normandie, at the mercy of futile directions from a lady-robot who was quite lost apparently somewhere beyond the Andelle river and deep in the heart of the Vexin, I suddenly saw, alone, rising from the level of the agricultural plain and seemingly lost in haze due to this hick country's humid climate, the Étrépagny sugar refinery's chimney rose towards the sky like a new steeple of Martinville. Literature. I didn't drive for long through this sublime text in which the beauty rose above the times I'm having to live in, for the barrages of beetroots lining ploughed fields where crows and gulls squabble over their borders had suddenly reminded me of the Nord-Pas-de-Calais and its similar tall fences set between two barbed wire landscapes built to do harm to Black people and other non-whites, to flatter the fascists and appease the English and all at the same time. With or without sugar, fine phrases are no good, this world is vile and my tragedy isn't making much progress. I feel bad because I'm alright, I'd like to do something in order to feel useful, but what?

I'm eating my strawberry jam on toast while the North Atlantic is facing the greatest threat to its borders since World War II. I don't know if it's moral, I'm thinking about immorality, for a long time I imagined a piece of literary buttered toast, I could see myself, through this ordinary toast, rediscovering a few seconds of my childhood, also toasty, it was a bildungsroman that smelled good the little green paths to skiving school, then I imagined the toast joining a collection of texts of which the semiology would contribute to the explication of our mythologies, or as one banal and ordinary element of a critique of everyday life, but that couldn't happen now, the times have moved on, there are no more childhood memories, myths are no longer found in objects and the present can no longer consist of a standard series of days and nights between one season and the next. At this juncture when armies are mobilising to join and reinforce the dissuasive and defensive stance taken on Europe's eastern flank, isn't the merest phrase involving the word 'toast' an insult to this North Atlantic I belong to? In these times when NATO has a finger in every pie, it may be acceptable, for example, to eat a slice of toast, but certainly not to build a whole literature around it. Hence I eat my toast and decide that my tragedy can wait, that all of literature can wait because there is a time for everything, a time for literature and a time for recovering one's strength, and it's with these words 'recovering one's strength', which I have from my mother, that I start to glimpse the possibility of an anti-literary use for a committed slice of toast. It is through my toast, yes, precisely with its strawberry jam, that I shall recover my strength! 'To recover your strength, you have to eat,' my mother used to say. 'Eat your toast, it'll make you strong!' – that's what she used to say and my mother knew what she was talking about; she is anorexic and has very little strength, she said you have to eat because she's incapable of swallowing anything. My mother butters slices of toast, she delights in the toast and gazes at the toast and ultimately foregoes the toast because she will always see something imperfect in the buttered slice. My mother's toastinal creation is a conceptual art. She will look at the toast and decide against it because the toast created is not the toast imagined but the reality right there in front of her, and then she's plunged into despair. Indeed this reality is *the essential object which isn't an object any longer, but this something faced with which all words cease and all categories fail, the object of anxiety par excellence.* Who spoke just then? I look around. No one here. This tale of torment makes me think of the war, of my mother's war and every war. Ever since childhood, my mother has had a horror of reality because of the war, she couldn't resist due to her poor appetite, she would have liked the appetite to eat and recover her strength and conquer the Third Reich. If she'd been eating when she was four, my mother would have repelled the Wehrmacht's Panzers single-handedly. Unfortunately for the world, she wasn't hungry. *The subject of the unconscious is only in touch with the soul via the body.* Who said that? But why would you want not to want what you nonetheless want? Who is smoking in here? I can smell something like cigars. Honestly, who is coughing and smoking round here? Shit, Lacan. How long has he been here?

'Hello, old chap,' I say. That's an expression from his youth, it makes him happy and also it's easygoing and I wouldn't want Lacan to think he might surprise me. Lacan always surprises me, of course, but the way he surprises me has ceased to surprise me. He comes, he goes, he comes back, he goes again, he is independent of my wishes, no one has ever influenced Lacan, no one can stop him from following his fancy. I'm glad he's here, of course, I'll admit that his fatherly style facilitates our transference, even though I don't find his tuppenny jokes funny anymore, especially since I've been working on my tragedy. Even though I'm not making much progress on it, I don't like being told it's the highest of high comedy, that's why I've stopped asking his opinion, and if he gives it anyway, I don't listen, except out of respect for the dead, besides I'm not reading him anymore. But that makes no difference, he shows up here the minute there's the slightest whiff of gunpowder in the air. The first time was back in 1991, he appeared mid-evening with his lecture notes in hand, his cigars and his weird shirts, to comment on the surgical strikes showing on a loop on my TV, then he launched into a seminar on the retouched photos in his style inspired by the purloined letter, and then he came back when my father died, in the middle of the Bosnian war. I buried my father, I changed a lot and then moved house, I thought I'd well and truly lost touch with Lacan thanks to a new and regular meditation practice, but he reappeared during Afghanistan, Darfur, Chechnya, Gaza, South Sudan, Yemen, the DRC, Syria and Mali, he's appeared and reappeared over and over, Lacan is a reapparition. When I think of war, I think of eating and of my mother and, as soon as I'm thinking of my mother, Lacan reappears to make his observations.

Anorexia is an imaginary without a body. This pre-supposes a body-machine that functions independently.

'Spot-on, old chap,' I reply, 'a body-machine. My mother has one that functions rather well. How about you – how are you functioning since your death?'

Lacan doesn't answer, he only likes his own jokes, he's sitting on the sofa, he looks well settled, he's in a kimono, I don't mention it, I also had my kimono phase. The kimono is the art of lounging around my place that Lacan seems to have developed at the same time as his passion for Japan, right after his Arabian Nights phase. Lacan gets these infatuations. First there was the Middle East, then Japan. He started buying babouches and Aladdin-style lamps which he eventually sold on in exchange for limited-edition Kiyonobu prints and Bashō haiku in the vernacular. His interest in Japan has no particular objective for he expects nothing of Japan, as he says again and again quoting himself, for Lacan is the king of self-quotation. When he quotes himself, it's because one must repeat what has been said again and again so that the re-saying works alongside the saying even while saying nothing more than has already been said, so he re-says *I expect nothing of Japan*. That's Lacan all over. *And the taste I have had for its usages, indeed its beauties, does not make me expect any more. Notably not to be understood.* Lacan in kimono expects nothing. Japan gives Lacan a holiday from himself. Lacan's holidays are almost always the same, either he goes to Japan or he comes to hang around my place in his kimono. Since he died, he seems to be coming to my place more and more often because, according to him and by his own decree, Japan is essentially a state of mind, hence it isn't necessary to go there in order to be there, whereas in kimono at my place, he can feel altogether in Japan. This is why, he said in his glory and without the least embarrassment, he likes it here and likes liking it and even revels in it. That said, however holidayfied he reappears, Lacan never stops doing Lacan and while I'm eating my strengthening toast and inevitably remembering my mother and I suddenly realise not only that I have a body but also that I'm in it, he's chewing my ear off with his tales of the bodily machine and describing the concept of the anorexic's soul as rejection of the Other at the mirror stage or something along those lines. I resist understanding, no matter, he goes on, he talks and talks while smoking and smoking unconcerned as to whether I'm really listening for, says he, TV or seminars or me it makes no odds, he'll as willingly talk to no one as talk to anyone for he, Lacan, is, quite simply, a talking being. However much he appreciates the Japanese temples and their invitation to silent contemplation, he won't stop talking and fully intends to go on as he always has.

It is very strange to be localised in a body, Lacan said while smoking. I wonder whether Lacan is aware of his personal lack of localisation in a body since he died but I don't raise it, I shouldn't like to annoy him, who would want to annoy Lacan? I nod and think about my tragedy, now that he's here and getting in the way of my getting back to it, I would really like to push on and even finish it, but Lacan must be pleased with his observation for he repeats more slowly, in case I hadn't yet grasped its true profundity, It is very strange to be localised in a body. I wonder if Lacan's seminars may not primarily be dedicated to his own stylistic satisfaction. I've never mentioned this to him, he has a horror of psychology; however, for someone so determined to stand as far as possible from his own discourse whose provenance, he says, is of no importance, he seems very pleased with these little formulae. Perhaps this is what gives him that air of pride that's so conducive to transference. I admit that I observe him and, yes, I envy him; I am not like him, personally I haven't the slightest poise, I come out with lines that are clumsy at best, I work hard at my tragedy, I write this or that, like this or like that, I know it's at the drama's conclusion that the actions will take on their true significance, then I reread myself aloud and weep, head in my hands, I compare myself, idiotically, to Sophocles, to Corneille or, worse still, to Shakespeare, and I end up demolishing all my lines one by one, until my whole tragedy is entirely dismantled, such that indeed it isn't, then, making very much progress at all. Lacan compares himself to no one and he demolishes nothing, he is always satisfied, everything he's said throughout his life adds up to much more than a book and nothing is to be thrown out. Since he's been hanging around my place expecting nothing of Japan or of life on earth, he is the great Lacan whose empire has grown and grown and whose glory... groan, likewise...I too have admired his hilarious puns, then I hated them, and now I couldn't care less, he's dead after all, I'm not going to change him, I offer him a coffee.

'Like a coffee, old chap?'

He prefers green tea, sencha ideally. All I have is English Lipton; he says, *Nothing then*. I ask, 'A glass of water?' He replies, *A glass of water is not nothing*. Then he falls silent, he stops talking, he's probably off to mess about with the structure of language, I count to ten, one two three people don't change four five six even when they're dead seven eight nine and the non-duped err, along with all the other ghosts.

If I say I want nothing to drink, I nonetheless do not want to drink nothing, he says to the bar at large, to his bistro company, doubtless, or to his drinking mates.

So what do you want?'

Pour me a glass of nothing.

I pour one for him. He thanks me and looks out at the rain over the town and the tree turning green.

I am sober.

'Well done, old chap.'

I am sober, which means...

I maintain an air of vague attention while watching him empty his glass.

...that I'm sober. Nothing more, nothing less.

I congratulate him again while giving the bar a little wipe down. Lacan has no interest in congratulations, what bothers him is the order of his speech. He is already deep in the notes he has scattered over the floor, but I'm not sure he's in a state to handle all the oratory art he's trying to prepare for because he's already said he's sober three times, which could cast doubt on his sobriety, and finally he admits that he hasn't stopped drinking for, says he, *No non-drinker could stop drinking that.*

He shows me the glass, I smile, I'm playing the game but I must say he's boring and I would now really like, if possible, to get back to my tragedy.

What does the non-drinker drink?

Tragedy presents individuals forced to act; it places them at the crossroads of a decision that involves every aspect of them; it shows their self-questioning, on the threshold of their decision, over the best course to take. I read that somewhere.

He drinks this!

'Reapparitions are not saints, you know,' I say while pouring him another little glass of nothing.

I shall go on with my tragedy, yes, one has to go on, never give up. But Lacan wants to keep talking, and when he wants to talk there's nothing to be done, especially when he's been drinking.

Anorexia is not a not eating, but an eating nothing.

He has that glint of the seminarist about him. He is glittering with a thousand sparks. Lacan's kimono is blue satin with a pale golden goose embroidered on the back. That's his taste – not much removed from wrestling fashion.

The soul without a body is perfection whereas the body without a soul is a machine and a machine without a soul is a poor animal. Lacan rarely laughs but when he does, it's always through his nose, in a way I call purely Lacanian.

Read Man and you'll understand.

'Man? What's that?' My ignorance tickles him.

Man what's that? Excellent question! Of course the great Lacan knows *all* about man, whereas I keep working on my tragedy forever and a day without making much headway.

Descartes, he says. *The Treatise.*

'I know that type, the type who read Descartes,' I say to Lacan because I remember those writers who knew everything about everything: read this, read that, read Descartes and then what? 'Is this how we can become less repugnant?'

Perhaps not.

'I'm working on my tragedy!' I say, to change the subject because I feel like crying, yes I do, suddenly, like crying with fury along with the teenage mums.

Very well, very well, he said. *Go on if you wish.*

Yesterday I heard about some Russian artists who've taken refuge in Berlin. They weren't singing any more, they said it had become impossible for them to sing, even sad songs, because thousands of people are being killed.

There is a time to sing, and a time to recover your strength, Lacan said, and looked at his watch.

He asked me for three hundred francs, polished off his glass of nothing and disappeared.

I sometimes feel as though Lacan can see inside my mind.

This story includes uncited references to works by Paul Éluard, Jean-Pierre Vernant and Pierre Vidal-Naquet, Marcel Proust, and Bertolt Brecht.

ANDRIY LYUBKA
ROASTED UGANDA

Translated by Yulia Lyubka and Kate Tsurkan

Andriy Lyubka is a prize-winning
Ukrainian writer who has published
ten books of poetry, essays, travel
writing and fiction. His debut
novel, *Carbide*, was first published
in Ukranian in 2015 and appeared
in English in 2022. He lives in
Uzhhorod.

Yulia Lyubka and **Kate Tsurkan**
are translators and passionate
promoters of Ukrainian literature.
In 2017, Tsurkan cofounded *Apofenie*
magazine, which primarily publishes
literature in translation.

OF ALL THE THINGS I TOOK TO THE FRONT for Ukrainian soldiers, the most important was a kilogram of freshly roasted coffee from a hipster coffee house in the centre of Uzhhorod. The package was rectangular and shiny, emblazoned with a stylish 'Roasted Uganda' sticker. It's something more suited for a post on Instagram than the front.

However, its primary function was defensive in nature. That coffee helped to protect not only the body but something even more important – it protected what made our soldiers human. Earlier, when I still wrote poems, I would call this strange substance the soul, but now, let it be the psyche. That coffee helped to protect soldiers' psyches because it made them feel that they were not just a piece of meat, a target for snipers and bombs, but people. They were still people with their own refined tastes, preferences and habits.

I recall that morning well. It was the start of May, when the nights were still chilly, but by dawn, the air was filled with warmth and fragrances. We were in a village somewhere outside of Slovyansk in Donbas, a village where there were three times more military than the remaining residents. The latter had mostly left as the outskirts of the village were being shelled almost daily, making it impossible to sleep at night due to the sounds of explosions. At night, you could hear them even more clearly; they gained volume and sounded ominously in the dark silence, like someone else's heartbeat.

That time, our volunteer team arrived at the location of the military unit too late. The checkpoint inspections took longer than expected, and the road was difficult. We got lost for a while on unfamiliar roads due to lack of a mobile connection, so we arrived at the location around evening, although it was not yet fully dark outside. This meant that we would be forced to spend the night with the military, as it was impossible to leave those places at night due to the light-masking regime. Online maps didn't work, the terrain was unfamiliar to us, and it was forbidden to turn on headlights. We could have accidentally driven into Russian positions in such a case. So we stayed overnight.

As we woke to the sounds of nearby and distant explosions, interrupting our short and restless sleep, we knew it was time to quickly set off for our next destination. But my friend, who after 24 February had donned a military uniform and now served in this unit, stopped us with a simple request: 'Wait,' he said, 'I'll make coffee.' Without electricity, he started the diesel generator, connected a small coffee maker to it, and filled it with water. He then took out a packet of coffee from the box I had brought him the day before. The label read 'Roasted Uganda'. He poured it into the coffee maker and within a minute, the May morning air was filled with the aroma of pure arabica.

I think that's how the Bible came to be written: people must have been just as surprised when Jesus began handing out fish and bread among them. It was a small miracle, to receive a metal mug of perfectly brewed espresso in the worst part of the world at that time, somewhere near Slovyansk in Donbas, in the midst of war. It may have been the most delicious coffee of my life. It sounds clichéd, but it's the truth.

With a knowing grin, my friend made a theatrical pause before responding to the unspoken question on our minds: 'What? I might die today. Why does it have to be the day where I haven't had my morning coffee? Fuck 'em, I have no intention of giving up my usual routine. No Putin will take that away from me. I start my day with a delicious espresso, and I'll be damned if I don't get to enjoy it just because of the war.'

After that, I visited various military units on fourteen occasions, from the north to the south, and from the east to the border of Russia in the Kharkiv region. I also went to the de-occupied territories near Kherson in the Ukrainian Black Sea region and to Donbas, which I now know almost as well as my native Zakarpattia. I saw, heard, and experienced a lot during these months, but that thought has remained etched in my memory. It resonates with something that is more significant than geopolitics, war zones and news reports.

Imagine a person who, until the beginning of the war, lived a peaceful, civilian life. They may have even been a latent pacifist. But after the full-scale invasion began, their life changed dramatically. They are now separated from their family, home, work, and plans for the future. They are dressed in a camouflage uniform, blending in not only with other soldiers, but also with the surrounding nature. Though they may be protected by armour, they feel exposed and vulnerable. They no longer have anything that defines them as an individual, as everything is now dedicated to a common, shared goal.

Another war soon emerges, the battle for the freedom to express oneself, to have personal preferences, and to hold onto daily routines, even if it means incurring significant cost. Having your morning cup of coffee is akin to returning home and spending time with loved ones – it's about being true to oneself. For a mere three minutes each day, one can set aside global agendas and state obligations, and simply focus on being unique and individual. This is what my friend believes to be a basic human right – the right to maintain one's individuality, to stand out and not be just another one of the millions fighting for their homeland.

This is another war, an unseen war for our personal time. I have heard from numerous soldiers that they actively read during their combat duties in trenches and dugouts. Specifically, they read books they had overlooked in university, as well as contemporary bestsellers on marketing and the history of business empires. They read because it gives them the feeling of not wasting their days, but rather using them for personal growth. The war takes everything from us, but one of the first things it takes is our time, our productive years, the period that we refer to as 'the prime of life'. It takes it irrevocably, so what can one do as a civilian, when finding oneself in the trenches, to not waste this time? That is why they learn German through Duolingo on their smartphones, read about the history of the IKEA corporation, or take driving lessons next to the battlefield. They read and study so that time does not feel wasted. I know it's a form of self-delusion, but it keeps a person going.

Maybe that's why I started visiting our soldiers at the front. In April, a friend of mine, who had recently joined the military, called me and mentioned that his unit needed a four-wheel drive vehicle. After the war commenced, the Ukrainian army grew sevenfold; soldiers were recruited, and they were given uniforms and assault rifles, but the equipment was lacking. They only had large trucks or old buses, instead of reliable, mobile transport.

Let me give you an example. A newly formed unit from my hometown Uzhhorod was sent to Donbas in early March. Since the division was newly formed, it lacked vehicles, save for an old yellow school bus. The distance from Uzhhorod to Donbas is farther than from Uzhhorod to Venice, so it's not surprising that the yellow bus broke down on the way. The soldiers waited for help in the cold for almost a day, but in the first days of March, the country was still in chaos, so no help was sent to pick them up. As a result, the soldiers – who, I remind you, were civilians just two weeks before these events – chipped in and drove the last two hundred kilometres by taxi at their own expense. A Ukrainian soldier going to the front in a taxicab is also one of the symbols of this war.

When I heard from a friend in the spring that their unit was in dire need of a jeep, I knew I had to help. I initially thought of reaching out to acquaintances or charitable foundations, but soon realised that no one would take immediate action. So, instead of looking for outside assistance, I decided to take matters into my own hands. That evening, I posted on Facebook that I was collecting money to purchase a jeep for a military unit in Donbas and provided my bank card number. To my surprise, by the morning, I had enough money for two jeeps in my account.

As if automatically, my current area of responsibility in this war was determined. I am no longer a writer, because I do not write anything at all. I collect money and buy cars for the Ukrainian army. Together with a team of like-minded people we repair them, paint them in camouflage colours and take them directly to the front. As of today, I have bought over a hundred cars for the Armed Forces of Ukraine and made fifteen trips to military units.

All of this was made possible thanks to the support of my readers, who have not only read my texts and come to book readings, but also financially supported my volunteer efforts. As a writer, it is a special honour and validation to see that the community I've built through my writing also trusts and supports me in real life. Though it may seem ironic, a writer who is no longer writing can also be considered a symbol of war. I sometimes jokingly say that readers are so eager to donate because they want me to focus on cars and not on writing.

Despite my current focus on purchasing and delivering vehicles to the front, I have a lot of material to write about. The convoy trips to the east usually take a day and a half to complete, so I have plenty of time to think and dream about my future writing. Specifically, I envision my first postwar book. It will be about everything in the world, but not cars. Once the war ends, I plan to buy a bicycle and have no further interest in cars because I'm fed up with them. I will make up for the writing pause forced upon me by the war by writing extensively about people, human experiences, situations, and voices. I will write about the war as a personal experience, not just as a geopolitical catastrophe. I will share about my initial fear and uncertainty of going from peaceful Uzhhorod to the frontline in Donbas for the first time, and how once I got there, I realised that fear is an internal concept, not a geographical one.

I will write about one of the drivers in our team, who was preparing sandwiches for us during a stop in Slovyansk when he cut his hand opening a can of food. Fifty years later, when his grandchildren ask him: 'Grandpa, what did you do during the war?' he will be able to tell them the truth: 'I can't tell you much. I will only say that I shed my blood in Slovyansk.'

The only thing I won't write about is a conversation with a soldier who came home on leave, who had drunk too much wine and confided in me, 'You know, there is only one thing I desire. This is an artillery war, which means that most of the time we sit in trenches and pray we don't get bombed. I've been at war for nine months and have yet to see a single Russian. So, I fear that a bomb will fall on me and I will die. I am not afraid of death, but I fear death by bomb, in my sleep, during lunch, at the table, or – God forbid – in the toilet. Bombs do not discriminate when it comes to how you die. I went to war accepting the possibility of death, but I ask for only one thing: if I must die then let me be killed by a man, let me see the enemy with my own eyes. May God grant me this last human grace: to perish at the hands of a man. Is that too much to ask?'

New Titles from Giramondo

Fiction

Shaun Prescott *The Town*
Jon Fosse *Septology* (trans. Damion Searls)
Shaun Prescott *Bon and Lesley*
George Alexander *Mortal Divide: The Autobiography of Yiorgos Alexandroglou*
Luke Carman *An Ordinary Ecstasy*
Norman Erikson Pasaribu *Happy Stories, Mostly* (trans. Tiffany Tsao)
Jessica Au *Cold Enough for Snow*
Max Easton *The Magpie Wing*
Zarah Butcher-McGunnigle *Nostalgia Has Ruined My Life*
Pip Adam *Nothing to See*

Non-fiction

Imants Tillers *Credo*
Bastian Fox Phelan *How to Be Between*
Antigone Kefala *Late Journals*
Evelyn Juers *The Dancer: A Biography for Philippa Cullen*
Gerald Murnane *Last Letter to a Reader*
Anwen Crawford *No Document*
Vanessa Berry *Gentle and Fierce*

Poetry

Lucy Dougan *Monster Field*
Michael Farrell *Googlecholia*
Lisa Gorton *Mirabilia*
Zheng Xiaoqiong *In the Roar of the Machine* (trans. Eleanor Goodman)
Lionel Fogarty *Harvest Lingo*
Tracy Ryan *Rose Interior*
Claire Potter *Acanthus*
Adam Aitken *Revenants*
J.S. Harry *New and Selected Poems*
Andy Jackson *Human Looking*
Eunice Andrada *Take Care*
Jane Gibian *Beneath the Tree Line*

For more information visit giramondopublishing.com.

Acknowledgements

We respectfully acknowledge the Gadigal, Burramattagal and Cammeraygal peoples, the traditional owners of the lands where Giramondo's offices are located. We extend our respects to their ancestors and to all First Nations peoples and Elders.

HEAT Series 3 Number 7 has been prepared in collaboration with Ligare Book Printers and Candida Stationery; we thank them for their support.

The Giramondo Publishing Company is grateful for the support of Western Sydney University in the implementation of its book publishing program.

Giramondo Publishing is assisted by the Australian Government through the Australia Council for the Arts.

This project is supported by the Copyright Agency's Cultural Fund.

HEAT Series 3
Editor Alexandra Christie
Designer Jenny Grigg
Typesetter Andrew Davies
Copyeditor Aleesha Paz
Marketing Manager Kate Prendergast
Publishers Ivor Indyk and Evelyn Juers
Associate Publisher Nick Tapper

Editorial Advisory Board
Chris Andrews, Mieke Chew, J.M. Coetzee, Lucy Dougan, Lisa Gorton,
Bella Li, Tamara Sampey-Jawad, Suneeta Peres da Costa, Alexis Wright
and Ashleigh Young.

Contact
For editorial enquiries, please email
heat.editor@giramondopublishing.com.
Follow us on Instagram @HEAT.lit and
Twitter @HEAT_journal.

Accessibility
We understand that some formats will not be accessible to all readers.
If you are a reader with specific access requirements, please contact
orders@giramondopublishing.com.

For more information, visit giramondopublishing.com/heat.

Published February 2023
from the Writing and Society Research Centre
at Western Sydney University
by the Giramondo Publishing Company
Locked Bag 1797
Penrith NSW 2751 Australia
www.giramondopublishing.com

This collection © Giramondo Publishing 2023
Typeset in Tiempos and Founders Grotesk Condensed
designed by Kris Sowersby at Klim Type Foundry

Printed and bound by Ligare Book Printers
Distributed in Australia by NewSouth Books

A catalogue record for this book is available from
the National Library of Australia.

HEAT Series 3 Number 7
ISBN: 978-1-922725-06-6
ISSN: 1326-1460

ISBN 978-1-922725-06-6